What's Up Doc?

→ Improving Work Ethics

: Establishing Work Practices for Productivity

Dr. Troy Looney

WHAT'S UP DOC?

Improving Work Ethics

DR. TROY LOONEY

ISBN-13: 978-1986604406

ISBN-10: 1986604403

DEDICATION

To every worker that gives 110% of their efforts to improving the work environment through ethical decision- making. Everything that you do is crucial to building character and reaching the goal of success and achievements. Continue to strive for excellence just by being that example of character and proper ethical standards!

TABLE OF CONTENTS

DEDICATION 1

FOREWORD..3

CHAPTER 1: INTRODUCTION...4

CHAPTER 2: THE ETHICAL MINDSET...............................6

CHAPTER 3. WHY ETHICS MATTER?.................................7

CHAPTER 4: WHEN ETHICS MATTER?.................................9

CHAPTER 5: BEING THE EXAMPLE...............................11

CHAPTER 6: MANAGING CHARACTER FLAWS 13

CHAPTER 7: SHARING YOUR ETHICS 15

CHAPTER 8: ETHICAL GROWTH 17

CHAPTER 9: ETHICAL CONCLUSIONS 19

CHAPTER 10: SUMMARY 21

ABOUT THE AUTHOR 23

FOREWORD

In the sense of ethics this can be defined as moral principles that govern a person's behavior, or the conduct in actions. This is synonymous with moral code, your morals, morality, values, rights and wrongs, your principles and ideals.

Taking all this into account when we speak of work ethics, how do you ethically perform at work? How do you behave? How do you react? How do you contribute to improving productivity? How do you support your co-workers and supervisors?

The more important question is: What do you do when no one else is looking? These are things to consider and reflect upon. Doing what is right morally and ethically will serve you well and present your character in a better light. This book is designed to improve work ethics. We are establishing work practices to be more productive. Providing a contextual reference for employees to increase and evaluate improved work ethics will reassure the administration that productivity can and will be enhanced to elevate the corporate culture.

Dr. Troy Looney

CHAPTER 1: INTRODUCTION

I would like to thank you for the purchase of this book which is the first in this series titled, ***"What's up Doc?"*** This book will begin by exploring what ethics are? What *ethics* mean? Ethics is the choice of right and wrong, and how we respond to those decisions are everything. ***Ethics** align with **morals*** and *morals align with our ethics (decision–making).* The question of ethics and morals are synonymous with one another and often used interchangeably. This book also asks the question: **how do we place ethics into context for improving work productivity and practices?** It is significant to state how important the role of ethics can be to the culture of the organization.

In **all organizations** it is crucial to maintain the highest level of *ethics and discipline.* This is accomplished by hiringthe **_right people_**that **_do the right thing_**. And not just sometimes, but **all the time!** In some organizations, the common place theme appears to be one of performing lazy until noticed. This behavior diminishes the entire culture of the organization. So, what if you have the entire organization acting with the same set of lazy mannerisms? ***You now have a problem!*** Of course we make friends and create friends in the workplace consistently. Those types of interactions are to be expected. Having better relationships simply means that you are approachable and liked by others. Relationships are built over time, and throughout a career pathway, you will establish some close ties with co-workers. All things considered, you still have to make good decisions by being ethical. It is good and bad to make friends because some friends can also be a thorn in the side of corporate culture when it's time to announce for changes in behavior. The perception of change comes with certain difficulties when it comes to discipline, but it is sometimes unavoidable. People are inherently resistant to change and will whine, cry, and fight for the right to refuse change if it disrupts their lazy and complacent behaviors. Well, what can leaders do to change the dynamics of these relationships through improving ethical decision-making? Time for change is to alter the perception of **"<u>Well that's my friend?</u>"** and get back to **"<u>let's do it right</u>"**. Let's discuss the mindset required.

CHAPTER 2: THE ETHICAL MINDSET

So what does it take to develop an **ethical mindset**? Is it the practice of trying to act accordingly, or is it something that one has already, and chooses to act appropriately to facilitate the morality of their character? Judging a person by their content of character is important to build a portrait of whom you are entertaining; however, the real test is in that **person's authenticity and morals**. It is not for us to judge their morality, but for them to reflect upon what choices they make in times of adversity and challenges. **It is important to think about doing what is right ethically,** then **make sure that you act on it!** It is our decision to be ethical when it comes to good and bad decision-making. Only we can select to perform at a higher level of morality. We must set the benchmarks to define our roles as professionals. According to Braswell (2017), **"Ethics is not about choosing to do right and wrong, but also doing nothing when we see others act unethically"**. We must constantly look at ourselves to reflect on actions and choices that we make. It is important to check ourselves to make sure that we are always considering our ethics as well as the ethics of other people. We are all diverse in our upbringing and beliefs, but we share the connection of community and social responsibility. Ethics are about holding ourselves accountable to people and to our community and our organizations.

CHAPTER 3: WHY ETHICS MATTER?

So why do ethics matter? They matter because the choices that are made can impact us indefinitely. Ethics matters because it should matter to you, your organization, and your employee's. **You should be the reflection to lead by example**. You should be the example for people to follow including your subordinates, your top, middle, and lower executive employees. **Ethics matters because if you're not going to do it right then why do it at all**. When there are opportunities for the organization to correct a clear violation or inappropriate action, I've heard many employees in organizations say, "Well, you know this place this? I understood that to mean that, "Well, this is how it has always been and it will not change, right or wrong." Multiple employees have noted how some companies takes care of certain people, and others they allow them to fail. Some organizations have also facilitated the demise and failure of some employees through the use of inconsistent disciplinary actions and punishments for errors not judged equally. In reality, the buddy system is not new. However, that doesn't make a correct. Wrong is wrong and right is right. Ethics are the choice between right and wrong. It should never be the premise of, "We like this person" so let's take care of them because that's the bosses' niece or nephew." What example are you setting for the company? Always display integrity at a higher level. Unethical actions create problems that may return to bite you later. We all have stories of favoritism entering into the discretionary decision-making. That is unethical.

All that employees can ask for is fairness. That is being transparent. That is leading by example. Anything else is unacceptable, and unethical. You should be willing to do what's right and be better than other companies. Expect more than other companies. Expect more from your employees. Expect more from yourself. That is called productivity and integrity. You show me the top successful companies and I'll show you will place where their employees say they love to work! When you set the example by reflecting a place where people love to work, you will get more from your people. **That essentially is an investment in your people**. If you value people as resources and understand people as being a resource of the company, then you will improve in every aspect of productivity.

<u>Employees can appreciate being treated fairly</u>, even in difficult situations. Morale suffers when people are treated differently from other coworkers in the same profession. If I make a mistake then I can deal with my discipline within the scope of what I understand to be appropriate for my actions. If I see another employee that violates a policy and makes the same mistake as I have, then I expect them to receive the proper discipline. If that outcome is not handled in the same capacity, then I have a problem accepting my discipline. **<u>Ethics is a practice that requires consistency above discretionary measures.</u>** That is why ethical behavior always matters.

CHAPTER 4: WHEN ETHICS MATTER?

<u>Ethics matters all the time</u>. Ethics matters when you have a chance to set the example of doing what is right and being correct in your actions. Ethics really matter when you operate with confidence and consistency. Ethics matters when you are fair and impartial. It is about making the proper decisions that are morally correct. I was thinking over a situation that happened in an organization, and just to preface what occurred I will give you an overview. Basically this organization failed to give credit where credit was due for outstanding work. Not just in doing the job, but doing an exceptional job and performing at maximum potential and achieving maximum results. In the seriousness of the matter, the organization treated a serious matter as an internal joke to ridicule the work of the actual employee; while promoting another supervisor whom was clearly incompetent to take all of the credit. **<u>Asking the ethical question of when ethics matter to do what is right?</u>** Even with understanding the 48 Laws of Power, it still speaks to ethics in action. It always matters. And it always comes back to reap the actions in the end. Even with the justifiable right to claim credit based on supervisory roles, the ethical and moral standards would be to acknowledge the efforts of giving credit where it is due, respectfully. This example reflects the lack of respect for an employee that clearly put forth the effort to represent the organization with clear distinction of meaning and character. **<u>You cannot act transparent and be a hypocritical</u>** in the same context. The truth speaks for itself and always will emerge into the light. The inability to correct unethical behavior by administrative decision makers, reflects the lack of proper leadership character, and leadership standards. **<u>Ethics, integrity, and respect must be earned; they are not deserved based on having a leadership title alone.</u>** <u>True leaders are based upon their level of influence</u> and how they represent and respect their position of authority. They must set the example at all times for themselves and for their organization. When ethics matter it should be represented with clear distinction and meaning at all times. **Not just to serve any agenda. Political or otherwise**. As it stands these actions were mitigated by other unethical practices, causing a larger problem for their agenda. Any administration that fails to support the ethical decision of doing what is right will always fail. The resulting outcome was also altered by corrective action toward the leadership, which has become the center of attention, based on other unethical actions. **Karma is a …..**" And with that in mind, I will leave you to develop your own inferences to fill in the blanks. Being **Ethical Always Matters.** Not only when the problems are illuminated and the attention becomes centered on you and your organization. There should be a standard practice of being confident in the decisions made prior to any problems. In this situation, the ethical decisions are a clear example of why you must be consistent. For those organizations that conduct practices that can be considered unethical, it is time to place them on notice. People are much wiser and smarter in this century of technological advancements and social media.

CHAPTER 5: BEING THE EXAMPLE

Just do what you know is right. If you truly know. I should preface my thoughts with the following statement. If you are the one that acts unethical in your organization, then you should be ashamed of yourself and decide on making a change to act ethically. Being the example to follow is really not that difficult. It requires a checklist of actions. Just be honest about who you are. You know right from wrong. It is borderline illegal in many cases. Be truthful about what you represent and what will benefit the mission of the organization. **It is important to improve work ethics by setting the example.** One idea to consider. It is crucial and essentially important when anyone enters a new field of work to have a mentor, or someone to follow. In essence the new employees should be properly "trained" on how to perform the job? So why wouldn't you have someone to set the example of ethical standards. The <u>mission of the organization</u> should be thoroughly understood and <u>introduced by a mentor that reflects the mission in accordance to the corporate policies</u>. Fair enough? So, how do you make someone set a good example? Particularly when being responsibly for teaching someone else, **<u>it is imperative that we transfer our highest ethical standards to them</u>**. This often becomes lost in translation, and of course if you are unethical, then more than likely, you will transfer your unethical practices to the mentee. In that case then let's go back to the beginning of this book and start over re-reading it from start to finish. This is about improving productivity and not diminishing ethical standards. Hopefully you know the difference between the two sorts. If you are puzzled as to what I just mentioned then, you should consider the next chapter of managing the character flaws. This chapter of the book was written and designed to help you break the cycle of practices that are unproductive or detrimental to the organization, and especially to your well-being. It is very likely that some people think they are being ethical, when in fact they are simply biased and judgmental against specific cultures, other than their own. Let's look at what creates character flaws in people, and how we might improve ethical decisions above your own ideologies.

CHAPTER 6: MANAGING CHARACTER FLAWS

Even with a flawed character, you can still be subjected to what will and what will not be tolerated. This is standard practice in most occupations. Another idea to consider is to carry yourself with a sense of humility over having a sense of superiority based on cultural differences or the likeability of an individual. Ethics should be decided by societal norms and not based on what some individuals feel are justifiable actions of entitlement to judge others. It is never acceptable to judge people and ignore your own transgressions based on ideologies shared by people with common interests. Basically, you should **have empathy for others** to set an example and understand our differences, while managing your own ego, and the egos of others.

Question? You might be wondering if all of these are inferences based on assumptions of experiences, and telling yourself, "What is he talking about right now?" Well, when I spoke about the entitlement factors, or having a sense of humility, I was simply introducing those individuals in leadership positions that have become a victim of their own egotistical values. Egos plays a significant role in creating the feeling of having superiority to others, based on a job title; status in the workplace; or perceptions. There are many things that can be corrected and managed but amongst the most difficult are character flaws and ego. **The balance is in learning to manage our flaws one character at a time.** Character is comprised of our backgrounds and our upbringing as we have been influenced by various experiences and lessons throughout life. Everything collectively is still our choice and our decision to do what's right and to make informed decisions. Trying to manager on character flaws is a very difficult task as a self-initiated ethical practice. <u>We must first know whom we are as individuals, and be honest enough with ourselves to acknowledge where we fall short within our character ethically.</u> From the management perspective of character flaws, we are accountable for making ethical decisions that require a more refined level of discretion and professionalism. The way that we manage people with character flaws is by sharing the corrected ethical standards. We must double check our own methods for flaws, to provide a proper foundation for cultivating character and better performance levels from people. For those individuals with character flaws, the best solution is to first recognize your weaknesses and work on changing them.

CHAPTER 7: SHARING YOUR ETHICS

When sharing your ethics comes to mind, the idea of decision making is almost synonymous with choices. The question here is; what will it take to improve work ethics and determine that you have the proper ethical standards to transfer to your subordinates? This means the evaluation of where your standards are outlined and the review of how these standards are aligned with the corporate culture, which resides in terms of the overall wellness of the agency. Taking into account that every company has different measurable outcomes in their practices, procedures, policies, and efforts, these ideas may or may not apply to your organization. When we recognize our flaws, and notice the flaws of other people, friends, and employees, the proper ethical decision to consider is to help them become better people. **We must establish our own higher level of ethical standards, and then share our findings** with other people to create an environment that we can all be effective and productive within. <u>So, how do you share your ethics?</u> Well, I feel that you can share your ethical standards in two ways that can be most significant to learn and practice between yourself and your colleagues. There are multiple ways to reflect on being ethical, but the two that appear to be most notable in decision-making are as follows: **The first way is to share your ethics with others by being the example.** Just be aware that you are always under the microscope and do the correct and right decisions. **The second way to share your ethics** <u>with others</u> is by letting them know when they have done something that is questionably wrong and unethical. This means to bring your "A" game at all times. You must be willing to persevere and find the strength and resilience to push through any and all obstacles. <u>You will be met with resistance</u>, but this is a part of any change that you attempt to instill or implement forward. People take criticism very personal, and you should exercise caution and professionalism when addressing situations that require you to address any issues of ethics. <u>The purpose of trying to share your ethical standards</u> are to <u>formulate a cohesive standard</u> that can be practiced on one accord for the organization. The purpose of this effort should be about uniformity, understanding and ethical growth.

CHAPTER 8: ETHICAL GROWTH

"Ethical Growth" is a phrase that I used to explain the purpose of this chapter. Growth in ethics means maturity of proper decision-making. **Growth in your maturity**, means better decisions that you can make <u>**without conviction of your character**</u> or the <u>**compromise of truths.**</u> With the mindset of improving work practices, we can start with how we increase the level of proper ethical decision-making. The goal is always for positivity to outweigh the negative issues that may arise. Tony Robbins (2018) said, **"Change is never a matter of ability it's always a matter of motivation".** The motivation to rise to the challenge of evaluating ourselves, and the motivation to evaluate other people for their actions can be demanding. In efforts to propose the challenge of building and improving ethics, all of us will be required to challenge ourselves for character integrity. However we set the examples for others, is the same measure by which we will see our ethical influences portrayed in the work environment.

Character examples being set for the organization are key components of ethical growth. It is crucial to note just how leadership's behavior and influence should always align with ethics and morals on a consistent basis. **Consistency is paramount** to have in all matters of being ethical and being an example for others to follow. In order to have an increased awareness about ethics, we must consider the changes and reasoning for justifiably implementing these changes. More often, the causes and reasons for changes are the direct result of something negative that may have occurred to create the need for improving practices. This can be attached to the motives that have created this sudden dynamic in ethical considerations and changes. The question to ask yourself is, **"What motives do you have for exploring the ethics in your organization?"** We must ask ourselves, what poor decisions have happened so that we now are commissioned to make changes and develop an awareness of our ethics issues? How might we instill changes prior to a critical incident happening? <u>The answer is to have focused ethical integrity in your efforts, while being transparent.</u> Transparency is required in all choices to reflect the organization in a favorable light with accuracy. Of course it is understandable to "get out in front of problems" by being open and honest about a new developing story. News is now reported at a much faster pace with the social media apps and reporting system. The proper perspective to these questions should be centered on the fact of having higher standards of ethical decision-making. By having higher standards, we might be able to avoid poor decision-making efforts in the first place. Again, consistency of efforts. We must learn to use our levels of influence to grow ethically in our organizations if we want to transform the culture of our organizations.

CHAPTER 9: ETHICAL CONCLUSIONS

Dwayne "The Roc" Johnson said, "Always be the hardest worker in the room". If you work harder than others, you will be rewarded with a reputation of being reliable and getting more accomplished. The "more" is about work productivity and practices that can always be improved, by improving ourselves. In seeking to understand how we might be able to improve work productivity through evaluating our work ethics, we should think, act, and assess three areas.

1. How might we **measure the current status** of our ethical standards, including ourselves and those around us that we influence?

2. What and if anything might have occurred to **increase the need** for this ethical evaluation?

3. Do we have the **correct policy and procedure** for implementing change as needed?

Each of these questions require several steps to address in accord with ethics. To measure the current status, we must first develop an informal protocol for assessment. **Measuring the status** of our ethical standards can be pursued in several ways. The easiest to review our ethical standards are in how we make decisions that will affect us. It is appropriate to consider the decision-making before any events actually occur, as to circumvent problems prior to them occurring. Think proactive in planning. The more <u>preventative maintenance/management</u>that you can offer, the better standards that you can develop for support of corrective actions. This constitutes the practice of being able to manage problems, without increasing your stress levels. We must keep the stress levels to a minimum so that we stay focused and think with clarity. As it might seem a little redundant to consider the re-establishing of your ethical standards with yourself and others, it surprisingly so has not been visited often enough. Evaluating the need for change is not necessarily the desired outcome, but improvement of productivity is always about making progress while in motion. Unethical behavior is typically enforced through policy and procedural violations. Policy and procedures are the written guidelines of enforcement for organizations. The rules that we formulate are what allows us to adhere to our corporate culture and expectations. When we find there are problems within our environment, the transparent thing to do is to address the issues directly, while focusing on corrective actions. In managing the problems and providing an alternative method of decision-making, the goal is to improve standards while getting more productivity out of that our people that are resourceful. Building our ethical standards for the organization and its administration supports the collective goal to achieve compliance. This book wad about the ethical standards in motion, but let's not lose sight of the fact that it deals with decision making by YOU! **You are the key to productivity!**

CHAPTER 10: SUMMARY

In the early section of this book, we explored the question of what ethics are and how we might come to evaluate ourselves and others for unethical practices.This book explored what ethics are in the context of decision-making with morals that are important to always do what is right, especially when no one else is around. The importance of discussing why ethics matter was identified to determine that you should make informed decisions to establish your character and consistency of practices. The question of when it matters to do the right thing is answered with "always". Administrative personnel are accountable with the responsibility in their roles of setting examples for others to follow. If you cannot set the proper example, then you certainly cannot evaluate others for their ethical decisions. You must understand the importance of managing character flaws that are identified. Once you can identify these flaws (starting with your own), then change can begin to occur. This is critical for progress in improving the culture of the organization. It starts and end with YOU, and your level of integrity and honesty. This ability to recognize character flaws will allow you to notice the areas of concern and implement the practice of sharing your ethical standards. Where growth and progress are considered, the intervention of problem areas can intercede as a turnaround strategy for change and improved decision-making. This will improve your productivity for growth.

THANK YOU FOR YOUR PURCHASE!

For Workshops and Seminars on Ethics
CONTACT ME:
DR. TROY LOONEY
LOONEY CONSULTING GROUP
www.LooneyConsultingGroup.com

ABOUT THE AUTHOR

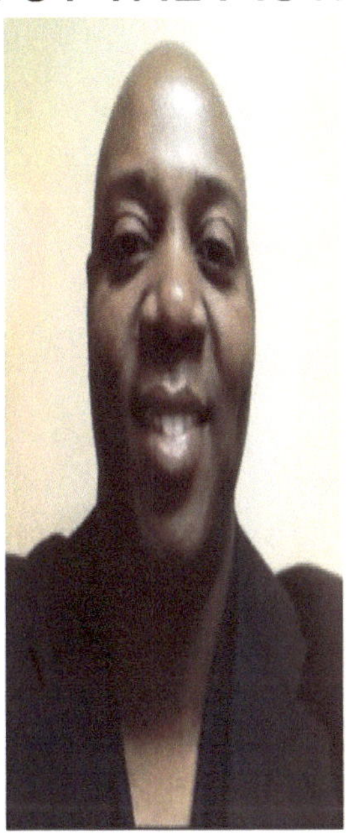

Dr. Troy Looney has written several books for the Amazon Kindle platform such as the ***"What's up Doc?"*** series. Each of these books are relevant to address readers in self-development areas such as: business, ethics, time management, self-motivation, and improving work productivity. Dr. Looney also currently assists doctoral and master level grad school candidates with NVIVO data coding, content development and understanding methodology in qualitative studies for support, guidance, and alignment. Dr. Troy L. Looney has a Doctorate of Management in Organizational Leadership, a Master's of Science in Internet Marketing, and a Bachelor of Arts in Business and Marketing. For more information on inviting Dr. Looney to speak at your next event, or to work one-on-one with Dr. Looney, please visit:

Thank you.

What's Up

Doc?

OTHER BOOKS IN THE
WHAT'S UP DOC SERIES

1.Improving Work Ethics*

2. Self-Motivation Factors

3. Finding Your Creative

4. Better Time Management

5. Being Relentless

6. Managing Messy People

7. Breaking Habits